DRAMATIC HOURS
IN COLONIAL HISTORY

The
Landing of the Pilgrims

BY

HENRY FISK CARLTON

Edited by CLAIRE T. ZYVE, PH.D.
Fox Meadow School, Scarsdale, New York

[1]

HOW TO BE A GOOD RADIO ACTOR

The play in this book has actually been produced on the radio. Possibly you have listened to this one when you tuned in at home. The persons whose voices you heard as you listened, looked just as they did when they left their homes to go to the studio, although they were taking the parts of men and women who lived long ago and who wore costumes very different from the ones we wear today.

The persons whose voices you heard stood close together around the microphone, each one reading from a copy of the play in his hand. Since they could not be seen, they did not act parts as in other plays, but tried to make their voices show how they felt.

When you give these plays you will not need costumes and you will not need scenery, although you can easily arrange a broadcasting studio if you wish. You will not need to memorize your parts; in fact, it will not be like a real radio broadcast if you do so, and, furthermore, you will not want to, since you will each have a copy of the book in your hands. All you will need to do is to remember that you are taking the part of a radio actor, that you are to read your speeches very distinctly, and that by your voice you will make your audience understand how you feel. In this way you will have the fun of living through some of the great moments of history.

HOW TO FOLLOW DIRECTIONS
IN THE PLAY

There are some directions in this play which may be new to you, but these are necessary, for you are now in a radio broadcasting studio, talking in front of a microphone. The word [*in*] means that the character is standing close to the microphone, while [*off*] indicates that he is farther away, so that his voice sounds faint. When the directions [*off, coming in*] are given, the person speaking is away from the microphone at first but gradually comes closer. The words [*mob*] or [*crowd noise*] you will understand mean the sound of many people talking in the distance.

Both the English and the dialect used help make the characters live, so the speeches have been written in the way in which these men and women would talk. This means that sometimes the character may use what seems to you unusual English. The punctuation helps, too, to make the speeches sound like real conversation; for example, you will find that a dash is often used to show that a character is talking very excitedly.

The Landing of the Pilgrims

CAST

PASTOR ROBINSON
ELDER CARVER
WILHELM KIEFT
VOICE
THOMAS WESTON
CAPTAIN JONES
PETER BROWN
MOB

ANNOUNCER

It was in the month of December in 1620 that the Pilgrim Fathers landed on Plymouth Rock and proceeded to establish the first permanent white settlement in New England. But the Pilgrims had not set out for America to establish their new home in New England—far from it—they had a charter permitting their settlement in the northern portion of the Virginia plantation, and it was toward Virginia that the little band of passengers aboard the Mayflower thought they were heading. The story of how they happened to come to the stern and rockbound coast of New England and of how they happened to stay there and carve out of the wilderness a great commonwealth is told here.

Let us begin our story in Leyden, Holland, where for some eleven years the Pilgrims have lived in exile from England, driven out because of their religious faith. It is early in the year 1620, and John Robinson, who is the pastor and leader of the Pilgrims, is talking to John Carver, who is one of the elders of the church.

ROBINSON

No word yet from Elder Brewster?

CARVER

Nay, not a word. I fear me that he and Master Cushman have found it impossible to raise such a large sum of money.

ROBINSON

If we delay much longer King James may repent himself of his generosity in allowing us to settle in Virginia.

CARVER

I begin to fear that we are doomed to spend the rest of our days in Holland.

ROBINSON

Nay, nay, do not lose heart. Jehovah will find a way for his children. Remember, the Children of Israel wandered for forty years in the wilderness before they found rest in the Promised Land.

CARVER

I'll not lose faith, Pastor Robinson. I know a way will be found for us. [*knock*]

ROBINSON

Will you see who's at the door?

CARVER

Of course, Pastor. [*sound of opening door*] Good day to you, sir.

KIEFT

Does Master John Robinson dwell here?

CARVER

Aye. Will you enter?

KIEFT

Thank you.

CARVER

Pastor Robinson, this gentleman would speak with you.

ROBINSON

Good morrow to you, sir.

KIEFT

Are you Pastor Robinson, then?

ROBINSON

I am. And to what do I owe the honor of this visit, Master—ah—?

KIEFT

My name is Kieft, Wilhelm Kieft, at your service.

ROBINSON

I am honored, Master Kieft. Allow me to present Master Carver. [*they greet each other*]

KIEFT

And now to the business that brought me here—it is rumored about Leyden that you and your company are about to leave Leyden. Is that true?

ROBINSON

There is, as yet, nothing certain, Master Kieft.

KIEFT

But you are planning an emigration to the New World, are you not?

ROBINSON

It has been talked of, certainly, but thus far we have not found the means.

KIEFT

Well, Master Robinson, perhaps I can find them for you.

ROBINSON

Indeed!

CARVER

Tell us, Master Kieft!

KIEFT

I am a member of the Dutch West India Company, which possesses a large tract of land in the New World.

ROBINSON

Indeed, I did not know that.

KIEFT

Ah, yes, through the discovery of a countryman of yours, Henry Hudson, who sailed under our flag, we own the country from the Great South River to the Great North River, where, I am told, the climate is healthful and pleasant, and the land rich and bountiful.

CARVER

And what do you propose to us?

KIEFT

My company is prepared to furnish you land upon which to found a colony, and capital to carry you and your people there and support you until you have made yourselves self-supporting.

ROBINSON

And for this you would expect of us—what?

KIEFT

Some small share of your profits.

CARVER

Yes, and what else?

KIEFT

Nothing, except that you should live under the Dutch flag and make our claim to the land secure.

CARVER

Your offer is generous, Master Kieft.

ROBINSON

And you make no other conditions than those you mention?

KIEFT

None, I assure you.

ROBINSON

Can you offer them in writing so that our people may consider them?

KIEFT

Indeed, yes, if you are interested, my company will make you a written offer within a fortnight.

ROBINSON

We are interested, Master Kieft, very much so.

KIEFT

Good. You shall receive our conditions as soon as I can arrange it. Good day!

ROBINSON

Good day, sir, and thank you.

CARVER

Jehovah has heard our prayer. The way is open. Mayhap—

ROBINSON

Is it not a generous offer?

CARVER

Generous? Aye, but still—

ROBINSON

Well?

CARVER

I like it not.

ROBINSON

Indeed, and why not?

CARVER

Why should the Dutch West India Company make us such a generous offer?

ROBINSON

Why indeed, but that we may establish for them a colony in the New World?

CARVER

Aye, a colony that will give them a stronger hold upon disputed land.

ROBINSON

Do you think the land is disputed?

CARVER

I know but little of the New World. I know not even where the Great North River or the Great South River may be, but only this I know: King James and his Virginia Company would take it much amiss, that having a patent to lands in Virginia, we turned to the Dutch and settled under their flag.

ROBINSON

And what has King James ever done for us but persecute us, drive us from our homes, and make of us pilgrims upon the face of the earth?

CARVER

Aye, but I am an Englishman. I had looked with joy upon our emigration to America, because I had hoped we could once again live under British rule.

ROBINSON

Many of our company have felt the same; but if we cannot go except under the Dutch flag, still we must go.

CARVER

Aye.

ROBINSON

The hand of Jehovah leads us; we must follow.

ANNOUNCER

So the offer of the Dutch West India Company was received and in due course of time the provisions were put into writing. The Pilgrim company discussed the offer from every angle. All of them would have preferred to settle under the British flag, if it could have been arranged, but because more than six months had passed and they had not found anyone who could finance them, they felt that the Dutch offer should be accepted.

Therefore, near the end of February, 1620, Pastor Robinson and Elder Carver meet with Wilhelm Kieft to settle finally the matter of the emigration. Let us listen as they talk together.

KIEFT

Two ships and one thousand pounds, which you can repay in ten years.

ROBINSON

And all your company demands is a monopoly in the fur trade?

KIEFT

That is all. Otherwise you shall do what pleases you; but all of the fur must belong to the Dutch West India Company.

ROBINSON

That seems just. What think you, Elder Carver?

CARVER

Who shall govern us, Master Kieft?

KIEFT

You shall say that yourself. Who governs you now?

ROBINSON

We have no governor except the Elders of the Church.

KIEFT

It shall be the same in the New World.

CARVER

Do the terms satisfy you, Pastor Robinson?

ROBINSON

Indeed, I am more than satisfied.

KIEFT

Then shall we sign the articles? [*rattle of paper*]

ROBINSON

I can think of nothing more we should consider, can
you, Elder?

CARVER

Nothing.

KIEFT

Then, if you have a quill, we can sign now. [*knock*]

ROBINSON

Your pardon, someone knocks.

CARVER [*going*]

I'll see who it is.

ROBINSON

Thank you, Elder. Ah, here is the quill. Now, where
is the inkhorn? Ah, yes, here.

KIEFT

Sign here. [*rattle of paper*]

ROBINSON

Let us wait for Elder Carver.

CARVER [*off*]

Oh, Pastor Robinson?

ROBINSON

Yes?

CARVER

Your pardon, sir, will you come here at once?

ROBINSON

What is it?

CARVER [*off*]

Thomas Weston of London desires to see you.

KIEFT

Can we not finish our business first?

ROBINSON

Tell him to come in and sit down while we get this business finished.

CARVER [*off*]

Will you come in, Master Weston?

WESTON [*coming in*]

Thank you. Have I the honor of addressing Master Robinson?

ROBINSON

I'm Robinson.

WESTON

I'm Thomas Weston, and I have come on behalf of a company of London merchants—

KIEFT [*sharply*]

Master Robinson, your pardon, but may we not finish this business in hand?

ROBINSON

Certainly! Elder Carver, Master Kieft is waiting for us to sign the Articles of Emigration.

WESTON

Your pardon, Master Robinson, did you say "Articles of Emigration"?

ROBINSON

Why, yes.

WESTON

I have an offer to make you for the emigration of your company.

CARVER

What?

ROBINSON

Indeed!

KIEFT

I must insist, sir—

ROBINSON

One moment, Master Kieft.

KIEFT

Are you going to sign or not?

ROBINSON

Master Kieft, this may cause us to change our plans; we must consider. What is your offer, Master Weston?

WESTON

A company of seven London merchants has agreed to furnish ships and capital to carry you and your people to America.

KIEFT

You have already agreed with me—

ROBINSON

We have signed nothing yet. Where, Master Weston, does your company propose that we settle?

WESTON

In northern Virginia—between the Great South River and the Great North River.

KIEFT

That, sir, is the land of the Dutch West India Company.

WESTON

Your pardon, but King James has decreed—

KIEFT [getting angrier]

I care not what your sovereign may have decreed—
he has no claim to that land. My company
discovered and explored it!

WESTON

Has your company established any plantations
there?

KIEFT

That makes no difference.

WESTON

Until you have established plantations, you cannot
claim it.

KIEFT

I do not wish to argue with you, sir. I am here to
close this business with you, Master Robinson. I am
waiting—

ROBINSON

We must have time to consider—

KIEFT

I had your word.

CARVER

Master Kieft, the situation has changed. We are Englishmen, and if we can emigrate under our own flag, you cannot blame us for preferring it to another.

KIEFT

You have tricked us—you are not treating me fairly!

ROBINSON

Now, sir—

KIEFT [*louder*]

And I warn you if you go to our land under the British flag, you shall regret it, sir, you shall regret it. Good day! [*sound of door slamming*]

ANNOUNCER

Thus the Pilgrims incurred the enmity of the Dutch West India Company, and though the terms of the London merchants were not so generous as those offered by the Dutch company, the Pilgrims accepted them and set about making their preparations for the great adventure.

They secured for their voyage two ships, the *Speedwell* and the *Mayflower*.

Our next scene is early in July of 1620. The *Mayflower* has been engaged for the voyage, and is lying at anchor in the Thames River off London, where it is undergoing some repairs preparatory to taking on cargo, which is to come to the New World. Aboard the ship is only the master, Captain Jones, when he is disturbed by—

KIEFT [*off*]

Ahoy, the *Mayflower*!

JONES

Ahoy! Who's hailing the *Mayflower*?

KIEFT

Here—alongside! May I come aboard?

JONES

What do you want?

KIEFT

I want to talk to the master of the ship.

JONES

I'm master. What do you want?

KIEFT

May I come aboard?

JONES

Come aboard. The ladder's over the side.

KIEFT

All right, I'm coming. [*lower*] Keep the boat alongside!

VOICE

Aye, aye, sir!

KIEFT [*low*]

Stay here till I'm ready to leave!

VOICE

Aye, aye, sir!

JONES

Here you are—right up here, sir. Give me your hand! Ah, there you are, sir!

KIEFT [*in*]

Thank you, sir. Are you the master of the ship?

JONES

I am, sir.

KIEFT

I understand you are engaged for the voyage.

JONES

That we are, sir, to America.

KIEFT

Aye, yes—by a company of London merchants.

JONES

And what's that to you, sir, begging your pardon?

KIEFT

No matter, I know well enough you are. And now, sir, I want to know if you'd like to put yourself in the way of earning a hundred pounds?

JONES

A hundred! Law, sir, and who wouldn't?

KIEFT

Exactly! I hoped I'd find you a man of sense.

JONES

What do you want me to do?

KIEFT

You are sailing for northern Virginia, are you not?

JONES

That's the orders.

KIEFT

Where do you expect to make land?

JONES

I was looking to make it in the mouth of the Great North River.

KIEFT

Hm—you know, I suppose, that the Dutch West India Company claims all the land bordering on the Great North River.

JONES [*laughing*]

Why, sir, everybody claims it. That's no matter. King James has proclaimed that all the land that has been settled belongs to them that has settled it; the rest is anybody's. When the company I'm taking gets their plantation settled, the Dutch can't claim the land any longer.

KIEFT

Perhaps not, but your company is not going to land on Dutch territory.

JONES

Eh?

KIEFT

You are going to lose your bearings—

JONES

Me—a sailor—lose my bearings?

KIEFT

Certainly—for one hundred pounds.

JONES

Well—

KIEFT

And you will make land far to the north of the Great
North River.

JONES

I'll have to see the color of the money.

KIEFT

Is it a bargain?

JONES

Have you got the money with you?

KIEFT

I have, and on your promise, I'll pay it.

JONES

All right. I'll see that the company is landed where
you wish.

KIEFT

Good!

ANNOUNCER

And so Captain Jones of the *Mayflower* was bribed by Dutch gold to play false with the band of Pilgrims. You know the story of the long and difficult job the Pilgrims had in getting fairly started on their voyage. The *Speedwell* sprang a leak, and they had to put back to Plymouth harbor where the ship was repaired. They made a second start, and again the *Speedwell* became unseaworthy and the captain refused to go on, so a second time the little flotilla put back to Plymouth. This time, since the season was far advanced and the Pilgrims feared that winter would be upon them before they could get established in their new home, the *Speedwell* was left behind, and on September 16, 1620, the *Mayflower* left alone for the New World. Halfway across the ocean the ship was beset by a long series of storms, so severe that it took more than two months for the ship to make the trip across the Atlantic. At last, on the morning of November 20, 1620, the ship's company were awakened by the electric cry of—

VOICE

Land—ho! Land—land—ho!

JONES [*calling*]

Where away?

VOICE

Two points off the starboard bow!

MOB [voices swelling up]

Land! Land! Is it really land? Captain, Captain! Have we really made land? Land? [*etc.*]

JONES

Aye, we've made land! Helmsman, bring the ship to bear on land, dead ahead!

VOICE

Aye, aye, sir, land dead ahead.

CARVER [*coming up*]

Ah, Captain Jones, at last!

JONES

Aye, at last—land ahead!

CARVER

Praise Jehovah!

ALL

Praise Jehovah! Amen! [*etc.*]

CARVER

Captain, tell us, is this Virginia that lies before us?

JONES

I know not; I've not yet taken our bearings.

CARVER

Do you not know where we are?

JONES

How should I? We've been tossed about in storms for a month, with no sun for days on end.

CARVER

There is sun this morning. Can you not take your bearings now?

JONES

The mate is figuring our position even now.

CARVER

Good!

VOICE

Captain Jones?

JONES

Aye, mate, have you the position?

VOICE

I made it, sir, about seventy west by forty-two
north.

CARVER

Forty-two north—but, Captain, we are bound for
forty north—we're out of our course.

JONES

What do you expect—with the storms we've had?

CARVER

Put your ship about—make for the south—this is
not Virginia!

JONES

We'll land here.

CARVER

We have no right to land here. Our charter grants us
land in Virginia, not here!

JONES

I can't help that. The ship is in bad shape—I won't risk sailing her any farther without repairs.

CARVER

Very well, you may stop here for repairs, but we must go on as soon as they are made.

JONES

It will take some time.

CARVER

My people will help you. We must speed the work.

JONES

Of course, I'll speed it all I can, but a man can't do any more than he can do.

CARVER

Well, get to it at once—this very day! We must get away from here within a fortnight or winter will be upon us.

JONES

Aye, so it will—and the winters in this country are bad.

CARVER

Then we must start south without delay.

JONES

Look you, Master Carver—

CARVER

Well, Captain?

JONES

Belikes 'twill be a month or more before I can make the *Mayflower* seaworthy—

CARVER

A month? Surely you can do better than that?

JONES

Perhaps not so well—why don't you land here?

CARVER

Here?

JONES

Aye. 'Tis a goodly country—full as rich as Virginia.

CARVER

Nay, nay, 'tis not to be thought on. We have a patent to lands in Virginia—a charter to establish and rule a plantation there; but here—why, the land is not ours—

JONES

It is if you take it—it belongs to no one else.

CARVER

But our Council would have no rights under the King—nay, nay. We go on to Virginia—as soon as you have made your repairs.

JONES

So be it, Master Carver.

ANNOUNCER

So the *Mayflower* brought up to anchor just inside Cape Cod, near the present village of Provincetown. The voyage had been long and arduous. There had been much sickness aboard, and Captain Jones knew that most of the passengers longed to set foot on solid ground and begin the task of building their homes. So he determined to create further dissatisfaction among them.

For our next scene we are going into Captain Jones's cabin just as one of the five men of the company, Peter Brown, has come into the cabin on the captain's invitation.

JONES

Sit you down, Master Brown, and find what comfort you can in my poor quarters.

PETER

Poor! If this cabin is poor, Captain, what do ye call what us folks has to put up with, all crowded into the common cabin like sheep er worse?

JONES

Aye, 'tis too bad the cabin is not a better place for your goodly company.

PETER

Aye, well, we'll soon be out of it.

JONES

I fear me, not so soon.

PETER

Indeed, why?

JONES

The ship must be repaired before we can go on.

PETER

How long will that take ye?

JONES

Mayhap two months or more, I know not.

PETER

Two months? Two months more in the cabin of this ship and half of our company will be dead.

JONES

Aye, belikes they will—and winter will be upon us hard and heavy. The winters in this country are worse than any you have ever seen in England or Holland.

PETER

Indeed!

JONES

The snow lies so deep it would cover a man's head—the land is blotted out, and even the sea freezes—

PETER

Then how could we get ashore?

JONES

I know not.

PETER

And once ashore, how could we find a fair place to build our homes?

JONES

'Tis not for me to say.

PETER

Why can't we land right here, Captain?

JONES

Because your Elder, Master Carver, says fix the ship and go on.

PETER

If Elder Carver says that, then there be naught that we kin do.

JONES

You'd stay packed in the ship's cabin, facing sickness and death, rather than rise up like men and tell the Elder what you will and what you won't do, eh?

PETER

Elder Carver and the twelve masters have the voice; we have naught to do but to obey.

JONES

Can it be that forty English freemen can't vote down twelve masters?

PETER

Under our charter the freemen have no voice.

JONES

Under the charter, eh?

PETER

Aye, so there's naught to do but what the masters say.

JONES

Have you never heard of mutiny?

PETER

Mutiny? Nay, we be lawful men, bound together in the love of Jehovah; we'll not mutiny! We must abide by our charter.

JONES

The charter, aye.

PETER

So there's naught to do—

JONES

Hold—have you thought on this—the charter binds you under the King's grant in Virginia Plantation—

PETER

Aye.

JONES

And you are not in Virginia—

PETER

Nay, not yet.

JONES

So you are not bound by the Virginia charter in these waters.

PETER

Forsooth, Captain, I'd not thought on that.

JONES

You have here all the rights of free-born Englishmen. And if you rise like men and demand that your Elders hearken to your voice, who shall gainsay you?

PETER

Aye—who—who, indeed? If we vote to land here, 'tis not mutiny.

JONES

Nay, 'tis but your right, if you want to land here.

PETER

We do—we do! Not a man in the company but would stay here if he had his way.

JONES

Then have your way—like Englishmen! Go to your cabin. Talk to the men of your company, tell them what I have told you.

PETER

Aye, Captain, I will! At once. [*going*]

JONES

Good! [*sound of door closing*] [*to himself*] Well, Elder Carver, we shall see whose voice is stronger—yours, or the voice of forty English freemen!

ANNOUNCER

Thus Captain Jones planted in the mind of one of the freemen of the Pilgrim company an idea which he was sure would bear fruit before many hours. He watched the company as first one man and then another fell in with Peter Brown. He felt the temper of the company changing, but he still did not feel that mutiny was likely against the strong religious authority of the Elders. And so to bring the matter to a head, he asked Carver to come to his cabin. As the door closes, the captain begins—

JONES

I fear me, Master Carver, we are in a bad way.

CARVER

Indeed—why?

JONES

The carpenter has gone over the ship timber by timber—

CARVER

Well?

JONES

It is a long, hard job we have before us.

CARVER

Oh, too bad, too bad! How long?

JONES

What with finding the proper timbers ashore, and hewing them to fit our needs, I fear it may well be two months or more before we can leave these waters.

CARVER

Surely you can make what repairs are necessary in less time—you need not rebuild the ship.

JONES

Nay—but the ship is sprung at every seam; 'tis nothing but good fortune that has kept it afloat so long.

CARVER

The seams sprung?

JONES

Aye—all of them.

CARVER

Then our stores are in danger of being ruined.

JONES

Aye, they are even now in such danger they should be unshipped.

CARVER

Then we must do it—set your crew to the work at once.

JONES

The crew has more than it can do to repair the ship and make it ready to sail on to Virginia, since you insist on going on.

CARVER

Then I'll set our company to work on the stores— we must not let them be ruined.

JONES

Nay, or you'll all face starvation, for you can count on nothing from the land at this late date.

CARVER

I'll gather the company together at once and set them to work!

JONES

Aye, do, Master Carver.

CARVER

We must unship the stores; [*going*] we'll begin at once. [*sound of door opening*]

JONES [to himself]

Mayhap your company will have something to say to that, Master Carver.

ANNOUNCER

So Carver gathered together his company in the common cabin, and standing before the stern-faced, storm-weary gathering, the Elder spoke:

CARVER

Men of the Pilgrim company, as no doubt you are all well aware by now, the land we made this morning with such joy and thanksgiving in our hearts is not the land of the Virginia Plantation.

ALL

Aye, we know as much! So we have heard. [*etc.*]

CARVER

But our ship is sore distressed from the buffeting of the storms, and Captain Jones must needs make repairs before we can sail on to our destination. [*protests and grumblings*]

I would it were not so, for I know how weary you find yourselves after the many days upon the sea. But there's naught else to do.

PETER [*calling*]

Why can't we land here? [*mob assents*]

CARVER

Nay, nay, it cannot be. This is not Virginia; we have no patent to these lands. We must sail on. The captain and his crew will make their repairs as soon as they can, but our stores in the hold are all of them in danger of spoiling—so we must needs unship them ourselves until such time as we may sail away from here. So let every man prepare himself for work.

PETER

Master Carver—we are not able to work. [*mob assents*]

CARVER

I know, but—

PETER

And more—'tis not our wish to stay aboard this ship longer—[*mob assents*]

CARVER

But we can do naught else—

PETER

Aye, we kin land here, and find a goodly place to build our homes and prepare against the winter that will be down upon us long before we kin get to Virginia. [*mob agrees heartily*]

CARVER

Men—men—quiet—hark to me! We've no right under our charter to settle here!

PETER

Then tear up the charter. [*mob agrees*]

CARVER

Tear up the charter? Have no government? Nay, we can't do that!

PETER

We be freemen, Master Carver; we have a right to a voice in what we'll do, and what we won't do—and we all want to land here, don't we, men? [*all agree*]

CARVER

But if we make our home here, we are outside the King's rule.

PETER

We'll rule ourselves—we be free-born Englishmen! [*all agree*]

CARVER

Mayhap—if that is your wish—

ALL

It is!

Aye, aye! [*etc.*]

CARVER

It may be for the best interest of the company and for the glory of Jehovah. I consent to your wishes. [*cheers*] But it behooves us to enter into a compact, one with the other—that no man may say, once we have landed in New England, that we have no law and cannot punish the disobedient.

PETER

May it please ye, sir, we be more than willing for the masters to write a compact that all can sign to be governed like any free-born Englishmen by the will o' the majority—[*all agree*]

CARVER

So be it—let the masters of the company join me in my cabin, and we shall make a compact joining all the company of freemen into a body politic. [*cheers*]

ANNOUNCER

And so in the cabin of the *Mayflower* the masters of the company, twelve in number, met in the first American legislative assembly and drew up one of the most famous documents in American history— the Mayflower Compact—which organized the first self-governing community in the New World.

www.ingramcontent.com/pod-product-compliance
Lightning Source LLC
Chambersburg PA
CBHW031614040426
42452CB00006B/524